COLLECTION MANAGEMENT

2/10/11	2 - 1	10/6/10

Prehistoric and Egyptian Medicine

Ian Dawson

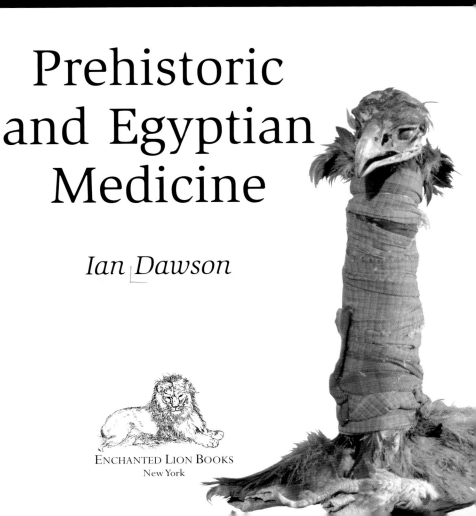

ENCHANTED LION BOOKS
New York

First American edition published in 2005 by
Enchanted Lion Books,
115 West 18 Street,
New York, NY 10011

Contributor pages 10–15: Kakkib li'Dthia Warrawee'a
Commissioning editor: Victoria Brooker
Editor: Deborah Fox
Inside design: Peta Morey
Cover design: Hodder Wayland
Picture research: Shelley Noronha, Glass Onion Pictures
Consultant: Dr Robert Arnott, University of Birmingham Medical School

Library of Congress Cataloging-in-Publication Data

Dawson, Ian.
  Prehistoric and Egyptian / Ian Dawson.—1st American ed.
     p. cm.—(The history of medicine)
  Includes bibliographical references and index.
  ISBN 1-59270-035-7
  1. Medicine, Egyptian--History--Juvenile literature. 2. Indians of North
America--Medicine--Juvenile literature. 3. Aboriginal
Australians--Medicine--Juvenile literature. I. Title. II. History of
medicine (Enchanted Lion Books)
  R133.5.D39 2005
  610'.901--dc22   2005043654

J 610.9

Printed and bound in China

Picture Acknowledgements. The author and publisher would like to thank the
following for allowing their pictures to be reproduced in this publication:
AKG Images 16, AKG/Ullstein 5, 8, AKG Images/Erich Lessing 33, AKG
Images/Francois Guenet 37, AKG Images/Andrea Jemolo 50; Ancient Art and
Architecture 46, 52; The Art Archive/Musee des Antiquities St Germain en
Laye/Dagli Orti 6, The Art Archive/Archaeological Museum Aleppo Syria/Dagli Orti
31, The Art Archive/Dagli Orti 32, 39, 41, 49 top and bottom, 54, The Art
Archive/Museo di Etnomedicina Piazzola sul Brenta/Dagli Orti 36, 60, The Art
Archive/Egyptian Museum Cairo/Dagli Orti 44, 53, 57, 58, The Art Archive/Egyptian
Museum Turin/Dagli Orti 42, 47, The Art Archive/Musee du Louvre Paris/Dagli Orti
3, 51, 55, 59; Butser Ancient Farm 24, 25; Centennial Museum, Vancouver,
Canada/Werner Forman 9; © Penny Tweedie CORBIS 10, © John Van Hasselt/CORBIS
11, Niall Benvie/CORBIS 12, E. O. Hoppe/CORBIS 14, © Richard Hamilton
Smith/CORBIS 17, Setboun/CORBIS 21, © Macduff Everton/CORBIS 27, 28, Diego
Lezama Orezzoli/CORBIS 34; © Gift of Mrs Joseph Harrison, Jr./Scala 19; Griffith
Institute/Oxford 56; Hulton Getty 23; Junker, H. 'Der Hofarzt Irj.' Zeitschrift für
Ägyptische Sprache und Altertumskunde, 1928, 63 tafeln II 43; Museum für
Volkerkunde, Berlin/Werner Forman Archive 1, 22; Peter Newark's American Pictures
18, 20; Robert Harding Picture Library 35; Rob Valentic/naturepl.com 13; Science
Photo Library 40, E. Strouhal/Werner Forman Archive cover, 45; Topham/Imageworks
4, 29, Topham 7.

Contents

Chapter 1

Medicine among the prehistoric hunter-gatherers

When was prehistory?

What ideas come into your head when you hear words such as "prehistory" or "prehistoric"? Many people might think, "that's the earliest period in history," but that belief is not strictly true.

Prehistory was not simply the earliest period of time. The word "prehistory" means "before writing." The prehistoric period lasted for different lengths of time in different parts of the world, depending upon when native peoples developed writing. For example, the ancient Egyptians developed writing around 3000 BCE and so that is when the prehistoric period ended in Egypt. In Britain the prehistoric period lasted three thousand years longer than in Egypt, until the Romans conquered Britain in 43 CE and introduced writing.

One major source of evidence about medicine and health in prehistory comes from peoples who continued to live as hunter-gatherers until recent times or still do so today. Here women of the San people of southern Africa are gathering edible roots. (photograph, 2000)

Evidence for prehistoric medicine

There are two main sources of evidence for prehistoric medicine. One is archaeological evidence, which comes primarily from skeletons that have been excavated and analyzed. The archaeologists can tell us, for example, about simple surgery carried out in prehistory (see p. 9). The other source of evidence comes from peoples who continued to live, or even still do today, in the same ways as their ancestors. Hunter-gatherers in Australia, Africa and the Americas did not need to change their ways of life because those ways were well suited to their environments, providing them with plentiful supplies of food. It was only the arrival of settlers from overseas that finally forced these peoples to change their ways of life.

Skeletons like these found at Yerevan in Armenia provide us with evidence of medicine and health. We can find out about the height and diet of the people and the condition of their bones can tell us about injuries, whether broken bones healed and the wear and tear caused by hard physical labor.

In other parts of the world, prehistoric conditions have continued. Peoples like the Khoikhoi and the San of south-western Africa still live similar lifestyles to their prehistoric ancestors and do not communicate in writing.

Hunter-gatherers

Many prehistoric peoples lived as hunter-gathers, though some eventually settled, becoming farmers. Most hunter-gatherers, however, remained nomads, never settling in one place. They lived in groups of fewer than a hundred people, following herds of animals for their meat and gathering fruits, plants and other food. This way of life provided the group with enough food to meet its needs, and also helped to protect their overall health.

The health of hunter-gathering peoples

The nomadic, hunter-gathering way of life protected people from many of the health problems that we know today. They did not suffer from infectious diseases, such as measles, smallpox and influenza, because these diseases only develop when there are large numbers of people settled together in one place. Nor did they herd animals or have domesticated animals, which later would allow for the spread of disease from animals to humans.

Another advantage of being constantly on the move was that the people did not stay in one place long enough to pollute water supplies or build up piles of waste, such as animal bones or human excrement, which attracted insects. They were therefore saved from the rapid spread of diseases that were to plague towns throughout the ages.

Prehistoric peoples hunted animals like these, which were painted on the walls of the caves at Lascaux, France c. 15,000 BCE. Many hunters must have suffered injuries that needed medical care and so people would have developed knowledge of the kinds of treatments that would help.

Dangers to health

However, life as a hunter-gatherer did lead to serious health problems. Hunter-gatherers suffered hunting injuries such as broken bones, cuts and bites, which could be fatal. Severe bleeding from wounds could be life-threatening. Bacteria in open wounds could cause gangrene or tetanus, which rapidly led to the victim's death. Diseases such as anthrax or rabies could be caught from animal skins or bites. Infections could develop from eating raw meat. Illness did not just endanger individuals living in groups of hunter-gatherers. It threatened everyone, because the group needed to follow the herds. Stopping to wait for one person to recover from a broken bone or an illness could mean that everyone went short of food. If hunter-gatherers took decisions in the same ways as modern hunter-gatherers, such as the Bushmen of southern Africa, then the whole group discussed sickness. In some cases, the group had the time or resources to feed and protect the sick person. On other occasions, he or she had to be left behind for the overall safety and well-being of the others.

A mother and child from Nabukeru in Fiji. Evidence from skeletons tells us that in prehistoric times women were in particular danger during childbirth, and it is likely that about a third of women died in childbirth in some societies. Women, on average, had shorter lives than men in all historical periods before the nineteenth century.

Average life expectancy

Life expectancy was very low in all early societies, largely because a quarter of children died before their first birthday. It is only recently that life expectancy has risen.

People	Life expectancy	Evidence
Prehistoric hunter-gatherers	19–25	skeletons/comparisons with modern societies
Early farmers c. 3000 BCE	20–27	skeletal evidence
Middle Ages (400–1400 CE)	22–29	skeletal evidence
UK 1861	40–45	census records
USA 1900	48+	U.S. Dept. Health & Human Services records
UK/USA 2002	75+	medical statistics

Treating common illnesses

How did prehistoric peoples treat everyday health problems? We cannot find the answers from skeletons, but the approaches used by modern hunter-gatherers and by the earliest farming societies provide us with clues about ancient treatments. Many treatments must have involved the use of herbal remedies, which were made up from the flowers and roots of plants. Herbal remedies have been used by every society in history.

Knowledge of effective herbal treatments was passed down through the generations. Over time, people learned which treatments to use for different medical problems by observing what worked and what did not. We now know, thanks to modern analysis of ancient herbal remedies, that some treatments would have had beneficial effects, because they acted as painkillers or they prevented infections. Other ingredients, such as cocoa beans from the cocoa plant or opium from the poppy, were used for their strengthening effect, which benefited the group, if only

The Aborigines used and still use the leaves of the tea-tree plant for medicinal purposes. People with colds or coughs breathed in the vapour from crushed tea-tree leaves boiled in water. People with fevers were bathed in the same tea-tree liquid. Today tea-tree oil is used to treat colds and other ailments and as an antiseptic.

for a short while, by enabling the sick person to return to work.

However, there were other reasons why certain plants were chosen to treat illnesses. Some were chosen for their symbolism, because the color, heat or shape of the plant resembled the health problem. For example, red plants, such as geranium or oil of St. John's Wort, were used to treat cuts.

Surgical skills

Prehistoric peoples developed simple surgical methods. They knew, for example, how to set broken bones so that they healed well. Most remarkably, there is evidence from as far apart as South America, the Pacific islands and Europe of "trepanning." This procedure involved using sharp flint tools to cut into the top of the skull to relieve pressure. It may have been done to release the demons that were thought to be causing the pain. The "trepanned" skulls show that the bones re-grew and that many of the patients survived.

Hundreds of skulls like this have been found, which show evidence of "trepanning." On occasion the piece of bone that had been cut out has been found, with holes in it as if it had been worn round the neck as a charm. This skull was found near present-day Vancouver in Canada and comes from the Marpole people who lived in the region.

Surgery – then and now

You might not expect prehistoric surgical methods to have been skillful, but they often were! As mentioned, there is plenty of evidence from prehistoric skulls of trepanning. One piece of modern evidence shows just how skilful prehistoric medicine could be. During the nineteenth century, a scientist travelling in the South Pacific islands watched a local healer, a medicine man, cut a hole in a man's skull in just half an hour. He used the same flint tools and methods as prehistoric people used. The patient was unconscious for several days but then woke up and recovered completely.

Aboriginal medicine

The indigenous people of Australia, the Aboriginal peoples, can provide some very interesting clues about prehistoric medical practices. However, like the medical practices of all cultures, Aboriginal medicine has progressed over time and is not the same medicine that was practised one, two or even ten thousand years ago.

Firstly, we need to understand just who the Aboriginal peoples are. Aboriginal means "the original inhabitants of." The Aboriginal peoples have continuously inhabited the continent and islands of the land we now call Australia, and they believe they have been there since the beginning of time. Archaeological and scientific evidence now suggests that Aboriginal peoples have lived there for more than 120,000 years. There are around 260 language groups representing about 700 nations, which means there are many different cultures and many different medical practices.

Aboriginal peoples had a wide variety of medicinal practices. This is because the Australian continent and its islands contain diverse ecological and geological habitats, each of which presents different medical problems and needs, and different materials to use as medicines. For example in south-eastern Australia,

A group of Aboriginal people living in the Northern Territory of Australia, photographed c. 1978.

jumping-jack ants can give a fatal bite. One Aboriginal treatment for this was to burn and inhale the smoke of a plant called "haboon," which soothed the allergic reaction to the bite.

Psychological healing

For Aboriginal peoples, psychological healing is as important as physical healing. They believe that everything in the universe is one. This means that if any part of the universe is sick, then other parts of the universe might also be unwell. Aboriginal peoples believe that if you and I are one, when you are sick, then I am sick too. If a kangaroo or a daisy-bush is sick, then you and I are sick. Aboriginal people believe that if you have an unhappy relationship at home with one person, you are unwell. This can lead to your immune system being sufficiently stressed for you to need medical help. In modern Western medicine, drugs might be used to boost your immune system, but from the Aboriginal perspective, you would continue to be sick as long as you had the problem relationship at home. In Aboriginal medicine, the emphasis would be on improving the problem relationship, and not on your immune system.

Aboriginal people developed great skills as artists, painting on tree bark and cave walls. Here the artist Kathleen Wallace displays one of her paintings while holding herbs used as medicines.

The concept of time

Where the West is governed by linear concepts of time, for Aboriginal peoples the present moment is all that really matters; after all, that is where you are. It is an interesting concept, because fear, anxiety and depression suppress immune function; they believe if you don't consider a future, you won't have fear and anxiety, and if you don't wallow in your past, you won't suffer from depression.

Preventative medicine

Perhaps the most important concept in medicine for Aboriginal peoples has been preventative medicine – *keeping* people well, not *making* them well. Aboriginal peoples live in a harsh, rugged and demanding land; if a person is sick in such a land, then he or she is a burden on the people around them. Yet, if people are well and kept well, the risk of such communal stress is significantly reduced.

Community elders

Each community had an elder, usually one of the older women who knew which herbs to use for various ailments. While most of the herbs wouldn't have been able to effect a cure, the elders relied on herbal remedies to relieve pain and to help meet certain needs of the sick person. Aboriginal peoples still believe that the cure must come from within the patient by attending to the problems that may have led to the sickness in the first place. This is one of the major differences between modern Western medicine and Aboriginal medicine. Modern Western medicine suggests that it is the pathogen—the virus or bacteria—then that causes disease. Aboriginal medicine says that the immune system can usually withstand the virus or bacteria, but if it is compromised and weakened by

In south-eastern Australia, Aboriginal peoples still use sphagnum moss as an effective dressing on wounds and cuts. Modern Western medicine has learned about the effectiveness of sphagnum which now is used in hospital dressings and in field dressings in warzones.

Snakebite

Often the people who caught snakes for food were the ones who had been bitten by snakes before. They had developed their own anti-venom within the body to survive the bite. Aboriginal peoples believed that if a snakebite victim could deal with the pain and shock, then the chances of survival were much higher. The bite was washed and the person went into a meditative state. This slowed the movement of venom around the body. Finally the doctors treated the pain with a herb called *Pratia purpurascens* or "Dtjidtjo'Krranyeahh."

spiritual, social, environmental or psychological problems, then the person may succumb to the disease. So, the patient isn't considered cured until the doctor, or medicine man, has treated the underlying problem that may have led to the disease, even if treatment by the elder seems to have resolved the immediate problem.

A Common Tiger Snake, one of the world's deadliest. These snakes are on average 3 1/4 feet long but can grow to nearly 6 feet in length. They live on frogs, lizards, small animals and water birds. Aboriginal peoples (see panel) developed effective ways of dealing with most snakebites.

Treating breaks and burns

If someone had a broken limb, then the Aboriginal doctor reset the break, making a splint from the bark of a tree. Then he bound sphagnum moss around the limb with the bark of the bootlace bush, known as "Mirrdturr'ain." A freshly cut sheet of bark from the thin, flexible eucalyptus tree was wrapped around the limb to keep it in place. The bark acted like a plaster cast, hardening to make a rigid support until the break healed.

Minor burns also were treated with the bark of a tree, the acacia tree. The bark was placed in cold water and the burn immersed in the water. The bark contains a substance called "tannin," which would form a skin across the burn, triggering the healing process.

Aboriginal hospitals

The Aboriginal doctor (the medicine man) was a practitioner of holistic, preventative medicine. He looked at the social, environmental, psychological and spiritual needs of people. As the Aboriginal population was very low and spread over a vast area, people had to travel great distances to see a doctor. Training doctors in Aboriginal medicine can take 20 to over 30 years. In south-eastern Australia, Aboriginal peoples had hospitals, so the communities knew where to find their doctor. In other areas people travelled great distances to visit the doctor, and doctors regularly visited communities. Hospitals were permanent structures where the doctor could look after the sick, the aged who could no longer keep up with their community when it moved from place to place, or the disabled.

An Aboriginal Medicine Man
c. 1930 in the Palm Island
Aboriginal Settlement.

The significance of "ceremony"

The Aboriginal doctor used (and still uses today) the power of suggestion to help patients find a way to cure themselves. This meant that there was a lot of cere-mony in the Aboriginal practice of medicine. Aboriginal doctors were masters at helping the patient make, through the ceremonial process, the physiological changes within their body that would bring about relief and cure.

Ceremony was very personal and it needed to illus-trate the potential cure to the individual patient and how it would come about. The practice of ceremony could include massage or smacking the skin to flood the area with prostaglandins to help relieve pain over the short term. It also could involve meditation to reduce stress and promote healing. Above all, ceremony needed to appear to be powerful medicine. It was the doctor's opportunity to create a "placebo" effect, by creating a sense of well-being in the patient without using medicine. Song, dance, smoke and water helped to inspire a sense of wonder about medicine.

Clevermen

The anthropologist A.P. Elkin called Aboriginal doctors or medicine men "Aboriginal Men of High Degree" or "Clevermen." He wrote:

My object has been to show, firstly, that Aboriginal medicine-men, so far from being rogues, charlatans, or ignoramuses, are men of high degree; that is, men who have taken a degree in the secret life beyond that taken by most males – a step which implies discipline, mental training, courage and perseverance. Secondly, that they are men of respected, and often outstanding, personality; thirdly that they are of immense social significance, the psychological health of the group largely depending on faith in their powers; fourth, that the psychic powers attributed to them must not be too readily dismissed as mere primitive magic and "make-believe," for many of them have specialized in the workings of the human mind and the influence of mind on body and of mind on mind ...

A.P. Elkin *Aboriginal Men of High Degree*, Inner Traditions International, 1993

Chapter 2

How effective was Native American medicine?

Evidence

Native American ways of life altered little over many centuries and the evidence of their medicine provides us with a second case-study of prehistoric medical ideas and treatments. Native Americans lived in many different ways, as there were around 500 different tribes,

or "nations." Some, like the Sioux on the Great Plains, lived as hunter-gatherers. Most, such as the Iroquois from north-east America, lived in settlements, collecting and growing crops but also fishing and hunting for meat. As the tribes did not develop writing, our evidence comes mainly from stories told orally by Native Americans themselves. The stories were later recorded or written down, along with descriptions of their ways of life that were written by European immigrants in North America from the seventeenth century onwards.

A seventeenth-century drawing by a French explorer showing various methods used by the natives of Florida to treat the sick. One man is sucking blood from a cut in the forehead. The man on the right breathes in the vapor from burning seeds.

Everyday remedies

Native Americans carried out simple but effective surgery to deal with injuries, such as broken bones or cuts. They sewed up cuts, using human hair, vegetable fibers or deer tendons. They cut off boils and abscesses and they treated snakebite by sucking out the poison. By using splints, broken bones healed well. For example, the Ojibwa (who lived near the Great Lakes) heated birch bark and used it to bind broken bones. As the bark cooled, it hardened, creating an effective splint.

A cherry tree in an orchard in Wisconsin, USA. Native Americans used the bark of the cherry tree to treat coughs.

Native Americans also treated many common illnesses, such as coughs and colds. Many of their everyday treatments involved making plants into medicines or ointments. Developed by observation and trial and error, they proved to be effective remedies. They boiled cherry bark, for example, in water and drank the "tea" to treat coughs. Today we know that cherry bark contains hydrocyanic acid, which helps stop coughing. Similarly willow bark was used to reduce fevers and pain; willow bark contains salicin, which is one of the main ingredients of the modern aspirin. There were many other such remedies, including the use of raspberry, elderberry, witch hazel, comfrey and echinacea. Around 170 of the Native American remedies are included in the official list of medicinal drugs in the USA.

Shampoo, the natural way!

Native Americans needed the same kinds of things we can buy in drugstores today, such as suntan lotion, insect repellent and shampoo. They used natural remedies. Native Americans rubbed animal fats and vegetable oil onto their skin to protect them from frostbite in winter and sunburn in summer. Bear grease was smeared on the skin to keep bugs away and some tribes even used urine as a shampoo to get rid of lice.

Health and hygiene

Native Americans were very clean, much to the surprise of many European settlers, who took far less care over hygiene. John Hunter, a prisoner of a native tribe for nearly twenty years, wrote a book in 1823 describing his experiences. In it he described how, among Native Americans, bathing "is much practiced, constitutes one of their greatest pleasures and contributes very much to strengthen the body. Men, women and children, from early infancy, are in the daily habit of bathing during the warm months and not infrequently after cold weather has set in." Native American homes were swept clean and some tribes burned the belongings of those who died, preventing illnesses from being passed on to others.

In the sweat lodges

Another common treatment was the sweat bath, which was used by tribes all over North America in their sweat lodges. In the center of the lodge the tribespeople

By daubing themselves with the juice from the purple bindweed plant, Native Americans from Carolina protected themselves from rattlesnake bites.

heated rocks in a fire until they were red-hot. Then they poured water onto the rocks to create steam; the effect was similar to that of saunas today. The members of the tribe sat in the heat and steam for as long as possible, occasionally running out to leap into a cold stream or lake. Sweat lodges were used for cere-monies or for cleansing the body, but they were used most often to treat illnesses, such as chest and lung complaints and also arthritis and rheumatism, which cause painful swellings of the joints.

Many early European explorers used sweat lodges and wrote about their effectiveness. William Bratton, a member of the Lewis and Clark expedition that first crossed North America in 1804–1806 to reach the Pacific, became so crippled by rheumatic stiffness and back pains that he could neither ride nor walk. He used a steam lodge and drank a native remedy – a strong tea made from horsemint – and soon was walking freely for the first time in four months.

A sweat lodge, painted by George Catlin around 1830.

Who used the best treatments?

Many Native American skeletons show signs of arthritis, which was often the result of carrying heavy loads. Tribes in the west, such as the Navajo, added crushed plants (such as juniper, sage and prickly pear cactus) to the water being poured over the hot stones in the sweat lodges. The combination of herbs, heat and steam certainly helped reduce the pain of sufferers from arthritis. European ideas were not as effective. In the late eighteenth century, the English missionary John Wesley recommended that sufferers from rheumatism wear washed wool of fine horsehair under their feet. German immigrants to America trusted in leaving their shoes turned upside down overnight!

A medicine man c. 1834 from the Mandan tribe, which lived in Dakota.

Medicine men

When an illness had no obvious cause, Native Americans turned to their medicine man. The medicine man acted as a healer by communicating with the spirit world that caused mystery illnesses. He could also be asked to solve or deal with other mysteries, such as predicting the future, telling hunters where to find herds of buffalo, casting spells, protecting the tribe from enemies or even going into a trance to "see" who had committed a crime.

The spirits and sickness

Native Americans believed that spirits, gods and demons were all around them in the sky, earth, rivers and animals, overseen by the Great Spirit, who had created the world. Therefore it was natural that they believed spirits were responsible for unexplained illnesses. An illness might be sent by an animal spirit, for example, if a hunter had not followed the right rituals before killing an animal.

Life as a medicine man

Once a young man had been chosen to become a medicine man, his training would last several years. He had to learn by heart all the chants, spells, dances and songs with which to communicate with the spirits. As a single ceremony might involve singing 80 different chants, many with 30 verses, there was a lot to be learned! He also had to learn about herbal remedies and to make all the equipment he would need for ceremonies, which included rattles, carved masks, drums, fans and spears. It was not an easy life. In most tribes the medicine man ranked second to the chief, but he was not allowed to marry and lived in isolation from the rest of the tribe. If his treatments were successful he would be well paid—in horses, furs, food or robes—but he would not be paid if he could not cure the patient. Sometimes the medicine man was beaten or killed if his treatments failed.

A drum was often used in healing ceremonies. Native American tribes believed that the roundness of the drum represented the wholeness of the universe and the drumbeat was a symbol of the heartbeat of the Great Spirit.

Choosing a medicine man

Some tribes said that if a young man heard a voice calling to him in his sleep and woke to see a mouse, he would become a medicine man. Mice were thought to speak all languages and were therefore messengers from the Great Spirit. In other tribes, medicine men were chosen because an animal summoned them in a dream to use their power for the good of the tribe. Such dreams could be the result of hallucinations caused by eating plants such as the peyote cactus. Other medicine men were chosen because as children they were often moody or daydreamed a lot. Women occasionally became medicine men. One who became well known was Sanapia (1895–1968), the last surviving Comanche eagle doctor whose life story was published in a book, *Sanapia: Comanche Medicine Woman* by David Jones, first published in 1972 by R&W Holt.

The medicine man at work

The medicine man's treatment began with prayer and meditation by going into a trance to learn what the Great Spirit wanted him to do and to "see" inside the body. He would chant his spells and sing songs, shake the rattle and bang his drum; all were ways of communicating with the Great Spirit. Then he would bring his tools out of his medicine bundle. He might use herbs, first chewing them and sometimes mixing them with water, then spitting them onto the open wound or the painful area. Some medicine men used tobacco, blowing smoke into the ears or nose of the patient to drive out the evil spirit. The medicine man might also massage or suck the area of the illness if he believed that the evil spirit had put an object inside the patient's body. Then the medicine man would produce the bone or other object from his mouth as if by magic and proclaim the patient cured.

This bundle belonged to a medicine man from the Crow tribe. The bundles contained animal bones, furs, wooden bowls, spoons, herbs and precious stones such as turquoise and green malachite, a source of copper. The Native American use of malachite is particularly interesting as it was also used in ancient Egyptian treatments and is now known to kill bacteria.

Diseases from Europe

Until Europeans arrived in America, native peoples did not suffer from smallpox, cholera, measles and many other diseases. This meant that when diseases hit, the tribespeople had no immunity. In 1837 two-thirds of the Blackfoot tribe was exterminated by smallpox. In 1849 two hundred Cheyenne lodges were wiped out by cholera. Indeed, disease played even a bigger part than the US cavalry in clearing the tribes from the Great Plains to make way for white settlers.

Recovery and belief

The medicine man's ways of working might seem trickery but his patients often recovered to some extent, if not fully, because their belief in the power of the medicine man was so strong. The herbal remedies they used also often helped. A third reason for their success is that many of the sick-nesses could be cured or eased. Evidence from skeletons shows that arthritis was a major health problem, while European observers noted that pneumonia, chest infections and digestive problems, such as dysentery, were also common. Cancer and heart disease however, were rare.

Mercy-killing

The tribes that lived by hunter-gathering, like other prehistoric peoples, would leave the sick and crippled to die in the event that they imperilled the whole group. Mercy-killing also was used to save individuals from the pain and misery of sickness. This partly explains why early European settlers marvelled at the good health and physique of Native Americans. One Dutchman wrote … "all are well-fashioned people, strong and sound of body, well-fed without blemish." However, the evidence as a whole suggests that many Native Americans lived healthier lives than the town-dwelling Europeans who ultimately drove them off their lands.

This stomp dance was performed to help a sick man recover. Tribes believed that dancing brought people into closer harmony with the earth and nature, and the soul closer to the Great Spirit.

Chapter 3

Medicine and health in the first settlements

The Neolithic Revolution

In many parts of the world—Africa, North America and Australia—people continued to live successfully as hunter-gatherers. However, in the Middle East and Europe, some peoples abandoned hunter-gathering around 10,000 BCE, at the end of the Ice Age, and began to settle in one place as farmers. The change from hunter-gathering to farming is known as the "Neolithic Revolution," because it took place in the period known as the "Neolithic" or "New Stone Age."

A reconstructed Iron-Age house built at Butser in southern England. During the Neolithic Revolution, people settled in houses. By the Iron Age *c.* 500 BCE, houses like this provided plenty of warmth and were carefully placed to make best use of sunlight.

People might think that the change to farming took place because it was a less dangerous way of life than following the herds. Yet that probably wasn't the reason. It is more likely that people were forced to change their way of life because they were struggling to find enough food. The population was gradually increasing and so more food was needed, but there were fewer animals to hunt. The numbers of animals such as elk and gazelle had fallen during the Ice Age when northern Europe was covered in glaciers. The first people to become farmers did so because farming gave them a better chance of survival.

Farming and health

Farming changed the kinds of illnesses from which people suffered. As farmers, people were in close, daily contact with cattle, pigs, horses and other animals. As a result, diseases that had previously affected only animals transferred to humans. Smallpox and tuberculosis spread from cattle to humans. Horses passed on many viruses, including the common cold. Measles, which still kills a million children a year throughout the world, originated in dogs and cattle. Animals also passed on bacteria such as salmonella, and their faeces polluted water supplies, spreading polio, cholera and other diseases.

Based on evidence from bones and wool fragments, Butser Iron Age Farm in southern England has established that soay sheep have been farmed in Britain for thousands of years. Nowadays a herd is kept at Butser, where archaeologists experiment with the kinds of farming methods used by prehistoric peoples to find out how successful they were.

A change in diet

Farming changed what people ate. Instead of eating a diet based on meat, fruits and plants, people ate cereal crops such as wheat and barley, which were made into bread. This type of food was high in calories but low in proteins, vitamins and minerals. The result was that people ate fewer nutrients, and diseases such as scurvy developed because people were not taking in enough vitamins. One result, which can be seen from the evidence of skeletons, is that people in the Neolithic period were a few inches shorter than their hunter-gatherer ancestors.

Medical evidence from the "Tomb of the Eagles"

Although people had begun to live as farmers, they could still be described as "prehistoric" because they had not yet developed writing. Therefore we do not have written records of their medicines or health. Instead we have to rely on archaeological evidence from excavations, such as the one on Isbister in the Orkney Islands, to the north of Scotland.

On a summer evening in 1958, farmer Ronald Simison was working on the clifftops at Isbister on Orkney. His digging unearthed an ancient wall and then, to his astonishment, a hoard of treasures that had been buried thousands of years earlier. These included a jet button, three stone axe-heads and a polished stone mace head. A few days later, Mr. Simison dug down further. He excavated what seemed to be a kind of room and there, in a tiny, roofed chamber, he suddenly saw a floor covered with human skulls. He had discovered the 5,000-year-old burial place of the prehistoric peoples of Isbister.

It was twenty years before the site was properly excavated and even then Mr Simison had to do it himself, having first learned as much as he could about

The site of the "Tomb of the Eagles" at Isbister on Orkney.

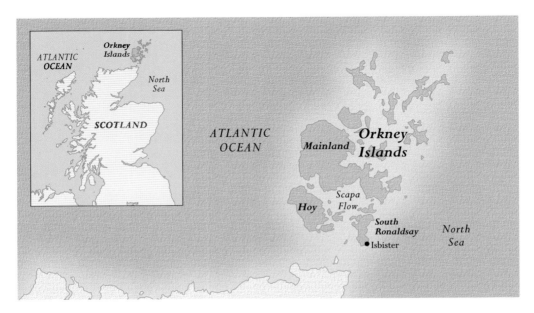

Ronald Simison inside the "Tomb of the Eagles," where he discovered the bones of the people who had lived there 5,000 years ago.

archaeology by watching other excavations and through reading. He unearthed around 16,000 human bones from the tomb. Painstaking work eventually identified nearly 400 individual skeletons among these bones. These skeletons give us a fascinating picture of the health of the people of Isbister 5,000 years ago.

A settlement of youngsters

If you travelled back in time to Isbister, one of the first things you would notice was how young the people were. The evidence from the skeletons tells us that there were three times as many people under twenty as over twenty, which is a very different proportion than today. We also know that 98 per cent of the people died before they reached the age of 40.

Burial of the eagles

Amidst the human bones in the tomb, there were large numbers of skulls and talons of the white-tailed sea eagle. When the excavation ended, archaeologists concluded that the local people had been burying eagles with their own dead for 800 years. One possible reason for this is that the eagle was a sacred bird to the people of Isbister. It led to the tomb becoming known as the "Tomb of the Eagles."

What the skeletons can tell us

The people of Isbister faced dangers to their health throughout their short lives. Their bones also tell us that one in five babies died before their first birthday and there was a high death rate among women in the mid-to late-teens, because they died while giving birth. On average, women died between the ages of 15 and 24, a little younger than the average age of death among men.

Although the people of Isbister died at what seem to us to be very young ages, they were not weak individuals. Their bones show that they were strong, with especially powerful leg muscles. They also had unusual bone developments around the ankles, which may have been caused by spending many hours squatting over cooking pots or by climbing the nearby cliffs to collect eggs and birds, keeping their ankles flexed for a good hold on the rocks. Some of the skeletons, mostly females, also show evidence of very strong neck muscles and they have a visible straight hollow across the top of the skull. The hollow was caused by people carrying heavy loads on their backs

A skull from the excavation at Isbister.

How tall were the people of Isbister?

The heights of the male skeletons ranged from 5 feet 2 inches to 5 feet 8 inches with an average height of 5 feet 6 inches. The female skeletons ranged from 4 feet 8 inches to 5 feet 3 inches with an average height of 5 feet 2 inches. The people of Isbister were therefore very similar in height to the peoples of Europe and North America in the nineteenth century but, on average, a few inches shorter than we are today.

and supporting the loads with a band stretched tightly across the top of their heads.

This kind of heavy labor left its marks on many of the skeletons. Most people suffered from osteoarthritis —a painful disease that damages the joints—caused by hard, physical work, such as carrying water. Even children had to work hard. The skeleton of a six-year-old shows signs of osteoarthritis in the back, the result of carrying heavy loads while still growing. The skeletons also show evidence of accidents, although very few indeed appear to have been fatal. Around two per cent of the people had broken a bone (a lower arm bone, an ankle bone, some ribs) and most showed signs of healing.

What we can learn from skeletons depends upon whether health problems have left marks upon the bones. For example, some diseases, such as leprosy, lead to changes in the bone and so can be identified. However, many other illnesses only affect the lungs or other soft tissues in the body and so leave no evidence for archaeologists.

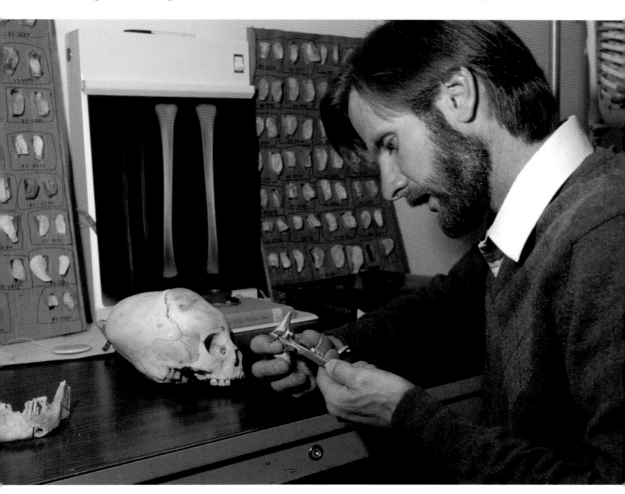

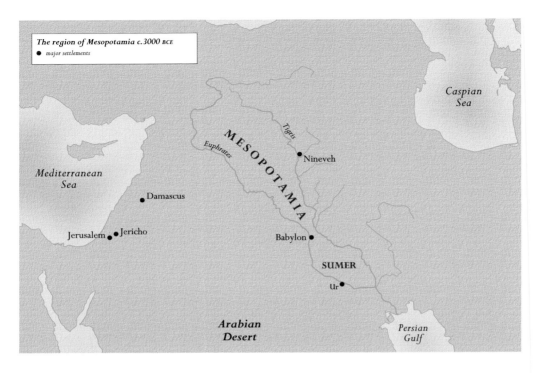

The region of Mesopotamia c. 3000 BCE
● major settlements

Caspian
Sea

Tigris

Euphrates

MESOPOTAMIA

●Nineveh

Mediterranean
Sea

●Damascus

Jerusalem●●Jericho

Babylon ●

SUMER

Ur●

Arabian
Desert

Persian
Gulf

New towns, new evidence

Evidence from skeletons, such as those from Isbister,
tells us how long people lived, what pains they had
and how fit they were. It does not tell us how the
people who lived in the first settlements dealt with
everyday health problems or what they thought caused
illness. The evidence that does begin to answer those
questions will only come from the first societies to
develop writing.

While the people of Isbister continued to live in their
small fishing and farming community, the first towns
were developing in the region known as Mesopotamia,
the "land between two rivers." The rivers were the
Tigris and the Euphrates, and Ur and Babylon were
amongst the first towns that developed around 3500
BCE.

Nowadays we think of town life and farming astwo
completely separate ways of life, but that was not the
case in these first towns. Many of the people there
combined work as traders and farmers on the extremely fertile land, watered by the two rivers. They

Mesopotamia, which means
the "land between two rivers."
This rich agricultural region
also became known as the
"Fertile Crescent" because of
its rich agricultural land.

grew abundant crops and this combination of farming and trade made the rulers and some of their people very wealthy.

The first medical records

The wealth indirectly led to new kinds of evidence about medicine. Writing developed because rulers, officials and merchants needed to keep a record of their wealth and possessions. The first evidence of writing comes from the region of Sumer around 3500 BCE. The earliest "paper" consisted of damp, clay tablets, on which the scribe, or note-maker, drew small pictures called pictograms, which formed the first kind of alphabet. When the scribe had finished, he placed the clay tablets in the sun, where they dried and baked hard, creating a permanent record. Gradually these writing tablets were used to record a wider range of information, including aspects of medicine, such as records of remedies and treatments.

The peoples of the different civilizations in Mesopotamia developed writing, giving us the first written records of medical treatments and ideas. This clay tablet from c. 1300 BCE is a contract for the sale of children.

The dangers of travel

Diseases spread further and faster as civilization developed. Life in towns became more prosperous and prosperity led to trade. Religions developed and so did wars. Each of these developments—trade, religion and war—led to travel, and travel spread diseases to new areas and peoples. We have little evidence from the earliest societies, but later examples tell us how deadly the arrival of a new disease could be. The Roman army first brought smallpox to Europe when it returned from fighting abroad. A handful of sick legionaries spread the disease among people who had no immunity. The result was around five million deaths from smallpox between 165 and 180 CE.

Medicine in Babylon

One of the most important sets of early medical writings comes from the city of Babylon in the time of King Hammurabi, who reigned from 1792 to 1750 BCE. At that time, Babylon was a majestic city with tens of thousands of inhabitants. The city walls were so broad and well-built that two four-horse chariots could travel around the top of them.

Hammurabi put down in writing a code of law that tells us about many aspects of life in Babylon, including medicine. The laws included instructions for physicians. They set out the fees that they could charge with a sliding scale that said that they had to charge noblemen more than commoners and commoners more than slaves.

The building foundations of the Hanging Gardens of Babylon, one of the Seven Wonders of the Ancient World. The Hanging Gardens were man-made terraces containing exotic plants and flowers. They were built on the orders of King Nebuchadnezzar (605–562 BCE) to please his wife, Amytis.

The causes of illness

Clay tablets from Babylon also tell us about people's thoughts on the causes of illness. Like prehistoric hunter-gatherers, the people there believed that the gods played a large part in both causing and curing illnesses and that illness could also be caused by an enemy's magic or by spirits invading the body. Some remedies therefore identified the demons that caused an illness and spelled out the chants to be said or the charms to be worn to help the sufferer recover. Healers also turned to astrology, by casting horoscopes or examining the entrails of an animal to forecast what the gods intended for the patient.

Herbal remedies

The records also tell us that the Babylonians used a wide range of treatments made up from herbs, plants and minerals. They used some treatments because experience showed that they worked. Senna and castor oil would have been effective laxatives, for example, and ingredients such as milk and honey may well have helped patients (milk because of its nutritional effects and honey as an antibiotic). In other remedies, the mixture of ingredients was linked to the belief in demons and spirits. Dog dung, for example, was used in mixtures to drive out the evil spirit causing the illness; another reminder of how close the medicine of the first cities was to the medicine of hunter-gathering peoples.

King Hammurabi's code of laws contained evidence about medicine in Babylon. It was carved onto this stone pillar, which is known as a *stele*. At the top of the *stele*, Hammurabi is shown on the left, standing before the god Shamash.

Cure him or die!

Hammurabi's law code laid down what happened if a physician was incompetent! A physician who operated on a nobleman and saved his life, for example, would receive ten shekels of silver (more than a craftsman's annual wage), but if he caused the death of the nobleman, then the physician's hand had to be cut off. If the physician killed a slave, then he merely had to replace him so that the slave's owner was not worse off.

The Great Bath of Mohenjo-daro

While the first cities were growing in Mesopotamia, similar developments were taking place in India. Farming settlements grew up around the Indus river, and around 3000 BCE the great cities of Harappa and Mohenjo-daro developed. Archaeological excavations at Mohenjo-daro give us an insight into some of the ways in which people tried to protect themselves against disease by building public-health systems.

4000-year-old bathrooms

Archaeologists exploring the ruins of Mohenjo-daro discovered a very sophisticated city. Four thousand years ago, the houses in the city had bathrooms made from brick and many had toilets. The waste water from the bathrooms ran along brick or terracotta pipes into sewers that were also made from brick and which ran along the center of the streets. The sewers were covered with stone slabs or bricks. To check or repair them, there were stones at regular intervals that could be

Brick-edged drainage channels along a street in Mohenjo-daro. Some houses contained bathrooms in which there was a small flight of stairs. Some historians suggest that a servant stood on the staircase and poured water over the bather to create a shower.

lifted. Solid waste was collected in sumps (large vessels), which were regularly emptied.

A system of cisterns and wells provided the people of Mohenjo-daro with supplies of drinking water. There were about 700 public wells and most houses also had their own private well. These facilities suggest that the people of Mohenjo-daro knew how important it was to keep clean and to drink clean water. However, the water supplies and sewers may have eventually caused more problems than they solved, perhaps leading to the downfall of the city.

The end of Mohenjo-daro?

The great city of Mohenjo-daro was deserted around 1500 BCE. Archaeologists are not certain why this happened, but from their excavations they have concluded that a combination of flooding and disease is the most likely explanation. The city was flooded as the Indus river changed course and destroyed low-lying houses. The floods also left stagnant water, where mosquitoes bred, leading to outbreaks of malaria. As a result the city became poorer because there was less trade, and so less was spent on keeping the water supply and bathing facilities in good condition. Mosquitoes soon began breeding in the city's drainage system and malaria became widespread. Water may also have seeped from the sewer system into the drinking water supplies, spreading diseases such as cholera. Eventually the city's people died or deserted their homes to live elsewhere.

The city also had a Great Bath, built on the citadel – the high mound overlooking the city. This was probably used for religious ceremonies and suggests how important cleansing was to the people of Mohenjo-daro.

The greatest killer of all

Perhaps the greatest threat to health created by settling in one place was malaria. Malaria has been described as the disease that has done "the greatest harm to the greatest number" throughout history. As forests and woodlands were cleared for settlements and to provide farmland, people created the ideal environments for mosquitoes, the carriers of malaria, to live and breed—warm waterholes, furrows and puddles.

Vedic medicine in ancient India

Around 1500 BCE, at the same time as the Mesopotamian city of Babylon was thriving and Mohenjo-daro was deserted, another civilization was developing in northern India. Historians believe it was led by the people who migrated to the Indian sub-continent from southern Europe and who spoke the language called Sanskrit. Its leaders were priests and they were the guardians of their people's religion, which was known as *veda*, meaning "the knowledge."

Vedic medical ideas appear to have been very similar in outline to those held in the same period in both Mesopotamia and Egypt. People believed diseases were caused by evil spirits or ill-luck but could be cured by the gods. They believed in many gods, each of whom was said to be able to cure particular diseases. The diseases most connected with the gods and evil spirits were those for which there was obvious, observable cause. These included *takman*, a group of fevers that developed during the monsoon (the

The face of the demon Vedda Sanniya, who was believed in early Indian medicine to cause the plague.

Buddhism and medicine

The Buddhist religion was founded by Siddhartha Gautama, the Buddha (563–483 BCE). The records of the earliest Buddhist monastic communities in India show that, although the monks were allowed very few possessions, they were expected to possess five simple medicines—fresh butter, clarified butter (ghee), oil, honey and molasses (a syrup or treacle extracted from sugar). Several hundred years later, around 400 CE, archaeological evidence suggests that these early Buddhist monasteries included sick rooms for the monks and so could have been amongst the very earliest hospitals.

seasonal heavy rains) and *yaksma*, which was probably consumption (a disease affecting the lungs). People appealed to the gods for help by praying, singing or saying *mantra* (incantations), or by punishing themselves to show their dedication to the god.

Alongside these beliefs in spirits and gods, however, the Vedic people used their own practical experience to treat everyday medical problems. Herbal remedies were commonly used as treatments, as they seem to have been in all early communities. Injuries such as broken bones were mended using splints. Open wounds or cuts were cauterized, which means that they were closed by applying a burning hot metal instrument or liquid to them – a method that was still being used in Europe in the 1600s.

A carving from a Buddhist temple in Angkor, Cambodia showing scenes from everyday life. In the center a sick person is being cared for.

Chapter 4

Medicine in ancient Egypt

Ancient Egypt – a wealthy country

The story of ancient Egypt is very similar to the origins of Mesopotamia. Farming settlements in the valley of the River Nile gradually grew into larger kingdoms until, around 3100 BCE, they united into one kingdom ruled by the Pharaoh, the god king. The ancient Egyptian civilization lasted for 3,000 years, due to its great wealth, which was based on farming.

Every year the Nile flooded as the rains came down the river from the Sudan. The floodwaters poured out over the river's banks, covering the land with rich, black mud that made the soil extremely fertile. The Egyptians learned how to dig channels and reservoir basins so they could retain enough water to irrigate the land during the hot season. This rich farmland

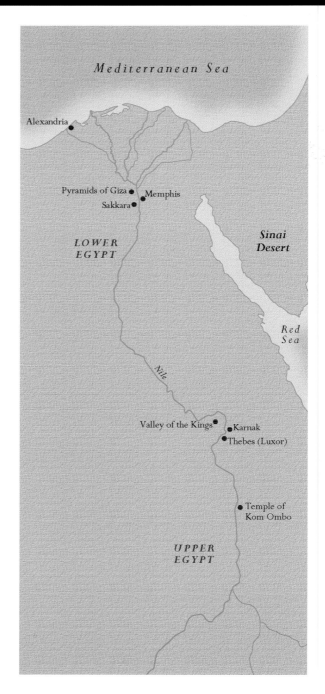

Ancient Egypt. The pyramids stand at Giza, but the Valley of the Kings, the burial place of later pharaohs, is hundreds of miles south, near the modern city of Luxor. At times, for instance during the reign of Ramesses II (1279–1212 BCE), Egypt conquered other lands, including the regions now known as Israel and Palestine.

produced wheat, barley, fruit and vegetables, and flax for making linen clothes. There were plenty of fish in the river and the Egyptian farmers herded sheep and pigs. They produced so much food that they could sell their surplus crops abroad, trading around the Mediterranean to Crete and Greece.

Evidence of Egyptian medicine

Like the peoples of Mesopotamia and India, the Egyptians had specialist doctors, took care over hygiene, used herbal remedies and believed that gods and evil spirits sent some diseases. However, we know a great deal more about medicine in Egypt than in these other civilizations because of the greater variety of sources that have survived and particularly because of the detailed written evidence preserved on papyrus, an early form of paper.

The Egyptians had two forms of writing. The most famous is the writing system using hieroglyphs (picture signs) seen on the walls of many temples and tombs. This system developed around 3300 BCE. A simplified system called "hieratic," which literally means "the writing of priests," developed later, c. 2500 BCE. This system was easier to write and was used on most papyri.

Wall-paintings, carvings and the inscriptions on tombs are major sources of evidence about life in Egypt, including medicine. This wall-painting from the tomb of Nakht, a scribe who lived c. 1400 BCE, shows the agricultural wealth of Egypt.

A doctor in hieroglyphs

The Egyptian word for doctor or physician was *swnw* (pronounced "sew-new"). Here you can see the hieroglyph saying *swnw*. It consists of three shapes – a man, a pot of medicine and a lancet. Taken together the symbols meant "doctor." Sometimes the man was shown leaning on a stick, which indicated that he was experienced and well-respected because of his age.

The medical papyri

The papyri, which give us so much of our evidence about Egyptian medicine, date from around 1800 to 1200 BCE. They were found during the nineteenth and early twentieth centuries by tomb robbers who simply wanted to sell whatever they found for profit. Unlike archaeologists, they did not record where they made their finds, so we do not know where these papyri came from. It is likely that some, at least, were found in the tombs of doctors.

Despite their origins, the papyri have surprisingly modern and "western" names. Some are called after the museum or city where they can be seen today (e.g London, Berlin). Others, including the most important, are known by the names of the men who purchased them from the tomb robbers. An American called Edwin Smith bought two of the most important in 1862. One, which is known as the Edwin Smith Papyrus, is 22 pages long. Smith later sold the other (the longest of all at 110 pages) to Georg Ebers, so it is known as the Ebers Papyrus.

A page from the Ebers Papyrus, which dates from *c.* 1530 BCE and contains 110 pages. It is written in hieratic script from right to left and provides the most detailed information about Egyptian medicine. We do not know exactly where it was found, but it may have come from the tomb of a doctor at Thebes, opposite modern Luxor.

Healers

There were three main groups of Egyptian healers – physicians, priests and magicians. The physicians would be those who come closest to the modern idea of a doctor as one who follows scientific methods. However, in ancient Egypt, there were many overlaps and similarities between magic, religion and medicine, and all three groups used many of the same methods, such as prayer or incantations.

Gods and medicine

Egyptians certainly believed that the gods were closely involved in medicine. Each specialization had its own god. For example, Dauw was the god of eye diseases and Taweret the goddess of childbirth. Gods too protected individual parts of the body – Isis protected the liver and Neith the heart.

A statue of the lion-headed goddess Sekhmet (the goddess of plagues) standing in the temple at Karnak. It dates from c. 1400 BCE. The funeral inscription of a priest of Sekhmet records, "I was a priest of Sekhmet, strong and skillful in the art. One who put his hands upon the sick and so found out; One who is skillful with his eye."

The priests of Serqet

There were groups of priests dedicated to each god. They performed the ceremonies of worship and prayer to the god. The evidence from papyri tells us that the priests of at least two gods, Sekhmet and Serqet, developed medical skills. Serqet was the scorpion goddess and her priests were regarded as particularly skilled in treating people bitten by scorpions, snakes or other venomous animals. Egyptians also asked the priests of Serqet to pray to her on their behalf so that she would protect them from scorpion bites.

Physicians

The healers who are described as "swnw" in papyri or in tomb inscriptions range from physicians at the royal courts to much humbler men who treated soldiers in the army or laborers working on Egypt's huge building projects. One of the court physicians was Ir-en-akhty – also known as Irj – who lived around 2100 BCE. Inscriptions in his tomb record that he specialized in eye diseases and also problems in the stomach and rectum. The Greek writer Herodotus provided evidence of the existence of specialist doctors; he visited Egypt in the fifth century BCE and reported ... "some [physicians] attend to disorders of the eyes, others to those of the head, some take care of the teeth, others with diseases of the bowels."

Among the other physicians we have evidence of is Hesy-ra, the first recorded doctor in history. He was an adviser to Pharaoh Zozer c. 2600 BCE and is described in his tomb as "chief of dentists and doctors."

A statue of Imhotep, the chief priest and adviser to Pharaoh Zozer, c. 2600 BCE, and the architect of the step-pyramid at Sakkara. Many centuries after he died, he became famous as a physician and was worshipped as the god of medicine. This statue was made c. 600 BCE, 2000 years after Imhotep's lifetime. Yet his tomb has never been found and there is no other evidence of him ever having acted as a physician! It remains a mystery whether Imhotep actually was a physician.

At the other end of the social scale were Renef-seneb and Akmu, whose names are recorded on a stone tablet listing over 100 people working at a stone quarry in the Sinai desert. They appear to have been employed as doctors for the quarry workers.

Women healers

We also have evidence of the first woman doctor in history—there is an inscription in what is probably her son's tomb of a lady called Peseshet (*c.* 2300 BCE). She is described as "overseer of the female doctors." The only other reference to a female doctor comes 2,000 years later (when Egypt had become part of the Roman Empire) when another woman physician, Tawe, is also named. Although there is little evidence, it is highly likely that mothers and other women in the family provided medical care in the home, just as in every other civilization. This was, however, such an everyday occurrence that it did not find its way into the medical papyri.

The "false" door to the tomb of Ir-en-akhty, the court physician. (False doors were created to try to deter tomb robbers.) The hieroglyphs around the doorway describe his many specializations, but also say that one of his roles was Inspector of Doctors of the Royal Palace.

Paying the doctor

The Egyptians did not use coins until around 350 BCE. Until then, physicians were paid with food, clothing or other daily necessities. A papyrus from *c.* 1165 BCE contains details of a payment by a man called Userhat in return for a physician's services:

1 bronze basin, 1 coiled basket, 2 pairs of sandals, 1 wooden rod, 1 basket with lid, 1 coiled basket, 2 jars of oil, some fine matting and a wooden object (possibly small furniture).

The papyrus does not say what the physician had done for his pay, whether he had treated one person or whether this was part of an annual salary for treating a group of workers.

What did the Egyptians know about the body?

We can obtain a good idea about how much the Egyptians knew about the body by simply listing the words used for parts of the body in the papyri. For example, there were plenty of words to describe the external parts of the body, such as the nose or neck, but very few parts of the skeleton had names, presumably because many small bones had not been identified. The Egyptians had words for the skull, lower jaw, vertebrae, ribs and collar bones—probably because these were the most obvious bones—but perhaps also because they were the bones most easily damaged in war or accidents at work. Similarly, Egyptian physicians had names for some, but not all, of the main organs in the body. They named the heart, lungs, liver, bladder and spleen, but not the kidneys, which are not in the abdomen and are hidden amidst fat.

The embalmed body, or mummy of Pharaoh Merneptah, who lived c. 1200 BCE. Embalming meant preserving a dead body in spices and wrapping it in bandages. The internal organs were removed and preserved and placed in jars (called "canopic jars"). Mummified is another word for embalmed. Mummies provide evidence of some health problems, such as eye diseases, arthritis and gall stones.

Learning about anatomy

Physicians did not learn about the body by dissection – the careful cutting and analysis of dead bodies— because religious law forbade this. It is most likely that physicians learned about anatomy whilst examining soldiers who had suffered open wounds in battle or workers who had been injured on building projects.

Embalming a body

Herodotus, a Greek historian who visited Egypt in the fifth century BCE, described embalming:

First they take a crooked piece of metal and with it draw out some of the brain through the nostrils and then rinse out the rest with drugs. Next they make a cut along the side of the body with a sharp knife and take out the contents of the abdomen. After this they fill the cavity with myrrh, cassia and other spices and the body is placed in natron for seventy days.

A wall-painting from a tomb *c.* 1200 BCE showing the god Anubis standing over a mummy. Egyptians believed that after death the soul left the body for a short time but it then returned and the dead person began the after-life. Saving the body for the after-life was a problem because it decayed very quickly in the high temperatures of Egypt. Therefore the body was embalmed.

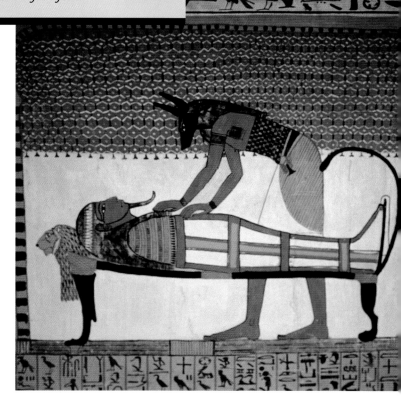

Historians still debate whether the Egyptians learned about anatomy through embalming. Embalmers may have spoken to physicians. There is, for example, a record of an embalmer who was the grandfather of a physician. However, the work of physicians and embalmers were entirely separate and, later in Egyptian history, embalmers were regarded as "unclean" and were cut off from contact with other people. Practically too, the whole process of embalming had to be carried out quickly, which meant that there was no time for careful observation of the organs. Overall, there is no conclusive evidence that physicians learned anything from the embalmers.

"May your channels be sound!"

The medical papyri tell us that Egyptian physicians believed that air, blood and the pulse were important for good health and that the heart was the most important organ in the body. The papyri warn doctors that it is a bad sign if the patient's "heart beats feebly." The Papyrus Ebers also contains a logical explanation of why the Egyptians thought the heart was so important:

"46 vessels or channels go from the heart to the limbs. If a doctor, priest of Sekhmet or magician, places his hand or fingers on the back of the head, hands, stomach, arms or feet then he hears the heart. The heart speaks out of every limb."

Medicinal oils were used to clean the body and so prevent illness. This carving shows two ladies pressing flowers in a container called a "ling" to make oil with a sweet-smelling perfume.

The idea that the body was linked by channels led to the development of a new theory on what caused illness. Egyptian doctors thought that the channels carried water, blood and air around the body and that this kept the body healthy. One daily greeting to friends was "May your channels be sound!" This idea may well have been linked to their observation of the River Nile and the irrigation channels that kept water flowing to the crops, which ensured a rich, healthy harvest.

A new theory about sickness

Egyptians knew that their crops died in the fields when their irrigation channels became blocked and were starved of water. They pondered too whether people also suffered if the body's channels became blocked. Therefore Egyptian doctors developed a theory that some illnesses were caused when mucus or undigested, rotting food blocked the body's channels and so prevented the health-giving air, water and blood from reaching the part of the body that was showing signs of sickness. While this was not the correct explanation for illness, it was an attempt to find a logical, rational explanation, rather than simply blaming the gods or the spirits.

The Egyptians also realized that cleanliness was important for staying healthy. This wooden box from the tomb of Kha, (an architect under Pharaoh Amenhotep II c. 1400 BCE) was, in effect, his bathroom cabinet, containing oils and other items for cleansing the body.

Observing the brain

Amongst the most remarkable Egyptian medical writings is this extract from the Edwin Smith Papyrus, which provides the earliest description of the brain:

If you examine a man [having] a gaping wound in his head, reaching the bone, smashing his skull and breaking open his brain, you should feel his wound. You find that smash which is in his skull [like] the corrugations which appear on molten copper in the crucible, and something therein throbs and flutters under your fingers like the weak place in the head of a child when it has not become whole.

Chapter 5

How did the Egyptians treat illnesses?

Treating everyday problems

Like other early peoples, the Egyptians developed a wide range of treatments. Some were linked to their beliefs in the gods, some were herbal remedies and others were practical treatments of everyday health problems. Women and other family healers knew from experience which remedies would be effective for minor health problems and these were handed down through families by word of mouth, just as they were amongst prehistoric peoples. However, the Egyptians' development of writing meant that they could also record treatments on papyrus. Their records helped to spread their ideas more quickly and have provided us with evidence of their methods.

A great deal of medical experience built up over time as doctors learned more of wounds in war, building accidents and simple everyday bumps and breaks. The medical papyri show that physicians were advised to follow a careful routine of examination, diagnosis and treatment, which is very similar to the routine of modern doctors. The panel gives one example from the Edwin Smith Papyrus.

Instructions for treating a broken nose

These instructions are from the Edwin Smith Papyrus:

EXAMINATION *If you examine a man whose nose is disfigured, part of it being squashed in, while the other part is swollen and both nostrils are bleeding.*

DIAGNOSIS *Then you should say "You have a broken nose and I can treat this ailment."*

TREATMENT *You should clean his nose with two plugs of linen and then insert two plugs soaked in grease into his nostrils. You should make him rest until the swelling has gone down. Bandage his nose with stiff rolls of linen and treat him with lint every day until he recovers.*

Surgery

Physicians also carried out simple surgery, removing swellings such as cysts and tumors just below the skin. The Ebers Papyrus, dating from 1500 BCE, contains instructions for doctors on how to deal with such swellings. It advises:

"When you come across a swelling that has attacked a channel, then it has formed a tumor in the patient's body. If, when you examine it with your fingers, it is like a hard stone, then you should say 'It is a tumor of the channels. I shall treat the disease with a knife'."

Improved metal-working skills produced stronger and sharper bronze surgical instruments, which helped doctors. Egyptian metalworkers had developed their skills whilst making embalming tools, fine jewellery and tools for the builders working on tombs, temples and the homes of the rich.

There are no illustrations of surgical instruments from the early periods. The earliest picture is this stone carving from the Temple of Kom Ombo, which shows surgical instruments from the second century CE.

This tomb carving of a wounded man, on crutches, walking towards a physician dates from c. 2300 BCE. Other tomb illustrations show injuries sustained on building sites, such as a mallet being dropped on a foot or stone chips getting into a worker's eye.

Herbal remedies

Egyptian doctors and other healers built up a wide range of treatments based on the use of herbs, plants, minerals and animal parts. These treatments were based on ingredients that could be found locally but, over time, more and more were brought to Egypt from further afield. Cinnamon, pepper and pomegranate came from India and China, saffron from Crete and malachite and yellow ochre from Chad in northern Africa. This widespread trade suggests that these items were highly prized for their medicinal use, although they may also have been used in cooking.

Despite the strangeness of some ingredients, many of these treatments would have helped the patients. People must have observed over many years what worked and what did not. Malachite, for example, was recorded in 39 different remedies, mainly for treating eye problems and open wounds. Honey was included in almost one-third of treatments. Modern scientific analysis confirms that both honey and malachite would have been helpful medical treatments because they help destroy the bacteria that cause infections. Other ingredients that attacked infections were myrrh, yeast (in bread and beer) and animal liver.

This tomb painting dating from c. 1450 BCE shows trading ships being loaded for a voyage. The voyages brought valuable herbs and plants to Egypt that could be used as medicines.

Some cures from the Ebers Papyrus
c. 1500 BCE

For a diseased eye

To clear up the pus: honey, balm from Mecca and gum ammoniac [gum ammoniac is the resin from the Dorema ammoniac plant].

To treat its discharge: red ochre, malachite, honey.

For diseases of the bladder

Rotten bread. The doctor must use it to fight the sickness, not to avoid the sickness.

For night blindness

Liver of ox, roasted and crushed out.
Really excellent.

A fragment of papyrus that contains "a perfect remedy." The medicine is made up from "one measure galena [lead sulphide], one measure honey and fat." Vegetables such as radishes, garlic and onions were given to workers at the pyramids as part of their pay. They all contain ingredients that protected the workers against diseases such as dysentery, typhus and cholera.

Mouse medicine?

Not all remedies were effective. One cure for baldness recommended smearing a mixture of fats onto the head —those of the lion, crocodile, ibex and serpent, amongst others! Then, mice were used for a variety of purposes, although we do not know why they were thought to be helpful. A mouse head was advised for treating earache, and a rotten mouse was the main ingredient in an ointment that stopped hair from graying. Skinned, whole mice have been found in the stomachs of the embalmed bodies of children, perhaps used as a last, desperate remedy. Although today people may view these "cures" with some bewilderment, it is worth noting that less than a hundred years ago, skinned whole mice were used in the English countryside for treating whooping cough!

Remedies for unblocking the channels

As the Egyptians believed that some illnesses were caused by the sufferer's channels becoming blocked, they naturally developed treatments that would unblock those channels. They included bleeding the patients— taking blood out of their veins—or making the patients vomit or empty their bowels. Yet these treatments did more to weaken than to help the patients.

The Greek writer Herodotus reported that "for three successive days in every month [the Egyptians] purge themselves … for they think it is from the food they eat that all sicknesses come to me." One cure for blocked bowels recommended mixing colocynth, senna and sycamore fruit into small cakes and feeding them to the patient. Another treatment recorded in the medical papyri advises what should be done for a patient whose arm hurts:

An Egyptian wall carving, showing a priest pouring medicine.

"There are two channels to his arms; if he is ill in his arm, let him vomit by means of fish and beer and bandage his fingers with water melon until he is healed."

A remedy for blindness

This remedy comes from the Ebers Papyrus. It shows the Egyptians' misunderstanding of the anatomy of the body and the importance of spells and chants.

A pig's eye, stibium, red ochre and a little honey are finely ground and mixed together and poured into the ear of the man so that he may be cured at once. Then recite this spell twice: "I have brought this ointment and applied it to the trouble spot and it will remove the horrible suffering. Do this and you will see again."

The scarab beetle was an important religious symbol for Egyptians. It was closely linked to the sun god who made life possible by ensuring the sun rose every morning. Jewellery in the shape of scarab beetles was worn as protection against illness or evil spirits. This scarab was made as a chest ornament for Pharaoh Psusennes I *c.* 1000 BCE.

Avoiding illness

The Egyptians' ideas about the causes of illness also led to a wide range of ways of trying to avoid illness. They believed that evil spirits caused some illnesses, so they used charms and amulets to scare away the evil spirits. Charms in the shape of scarab beetles were especially popular, particularly amongst the rich who could afford them. Poorer families made do with homemade charms. One such charm, made by a mother to protect her child, mixed the effectiveness of herbal remedies with the belief in charms and spirits:

"I have made a charm for my child which will protect him against you, oh evil spirits! This charm is made from evil smelling herbs and from garlic which is harmful to you; from honey which is sweet for men and horrible for spirits, from a fishtail and a rag and a backbone of a perch."

Hygiene and health

Herodotus was also impressed by the Egyptians'
personal hygiene. He noted that they drank from bronze
cups that were cleaned everyday, that they always wore
newly washed linen clothing and that they washed
twice a day and every night in cold water. Their priests
shaved themselves every third day so that no lice would
"infest them while they are in the service of the gods."
Other records prove that Herodotus was right in
praising Egyptian cleanliness. Rich and poor people
did wash regularly, including before meals. They used
soda, scented oil and ointments as soap. Egyptian
ladies shaved their bodies with bronze razors and used
eye make-up that contained powdered emerald-green
copper ore, which may well have helped to reduce
eye-infections, although that was probably not why
they wore it!

A wall-painting from the tomb
of Nakht, a scribe who lived
c. 1400 BCE, showing Egyptian
ladies washing. Both rich and
poor people washed often.

Toilets and keeping clean

Excavations by archaeologists tell us about hygiene in people's homes. Kahun was a settlement of 5,000 people who were working on a pyramid for Pharaoh Sesostris II around 1900 BCE. The richer homes contained a room for washing and bathing, but they did not have a complex plumbing system to bring water in and out. People bathed by sitting or standing on a stone slab while a servant poured water over them from a jug. The waste water ran away through a hole in the wall, draining into a sunken vessel in the floor or into stone drains in the street.

Workers in poorer homes washed in stone tanks set into the mud floors. They also had simple toilets—a wooden stool with a hole cut into it above a container half-filled with sand. Richer families used a limestone toilet seat placed over a bowl that stood in a pit. Whatever kind of toilet they had, they all had to be emptied by hand.

An amulet of Taweret, the goddess of childbirth, worn by women while they were pregnant. Taweret was a pregnant hippopotamus! She was always shown looking particularly fierce to make sure that evil spirits were frightened away.

The first mosquito nets

Some methods used by the Egyptians to avoid illness were based on very practical ideas. In the fifth century BCE, Herodotus noted:

"Gnats are abundant. This is how the Egyptians protect themselves against them. Each man possesses a net. By day it is used to catch fish but at night he spreads it over his bed and goes to sleep underneath. If he rolls himself in a piece of muslin the gnats can bite through that but they do not attempt to get through the net."

Chapter 6

How successful was prehistoric and Egyptian medicine?

Some interesting cures

To cure whooping cough, ride a donkey seven times in a circle or crawl under the donkey seven times.

To cure tuberculosis, breathe into a freshly dug hole in the ground or swallow live snails.

To cure epilepsy, take the skull of a young woman, pound it into small bits, mix it with treacle and take it in small doses.

How effective were the cures

If you read the panel, you might laugh and say that overall early cures must not have done much good. Yet those same cures actually were used by people in England in the nineteenth century, at the same time as scientists were making discoveries about anaesthetics, antiseptics and bacteria—the true cause of disease. All societies throughout the world have had a mix of effective medical treatments and ideas that simply did not work!

This wall-painting from *c.* 1450 BCE shows a Syrian prince (seated) consulting the Egyptian physician Nebamon, another example of how medical ideas spread. Nebamon appears to be handing a medicine to his patient.

What were the strengths of ancient medicine? Perhaps the greatest were treatments using herbs, plants and minerals. Thanks to scientific analysis, we know that honey and malachite reduce infections, but ancient peoples had to discover this by trial and error. Trade helped spread good ideas, with herbs being sent from India to Egypt and from north Africa across the Mediterranean.

Dealing with accidents

Ancient peoples also developed good methods of dealing with accidents, making splints, for example, which kept bones straight while they healed. Simple surgery was carried out, using different kinds of thread to close up wounds. Surgeons gained experience of this work during times of war, and war also helped improve metalworking skills, because soldiers wanted better weapons. In time this led to surgeons having sharper blades and finer instruments to use.

Specialist doctors and medicine men

Early societies also saw the arrival of the first specialist doctors, who developed knowledge of the major organs in the body and tried to work out why people became ill. They knew that many illnesses had everyday causes. What happened though when there was no obvious cause? Then people turned to their medicine man or priest. People all over the world explained mysterious illnesses in the same ways. They believed that illnesses were sent by the gods as a punishment or by an enemy who had attacked the sufferer's spirit. These ideas might seem unusual today, but it is only 150 years since scientists discovered the real cause of disease. How else could people have explained diseases, other than to blame the gods?

A model of Seneb and his family, from his tomb *c.* 2500 BCE. Seneb suffered from a type of dwarfism but lived a respected life as a high-ranking official in the Pharaoh's palace.

How long did people live for?

Ancient peoples had much shorter lives than people in western Europe and America today. The evidence from skeletons shows that few people in prehistoric times would have lived beyond the age of 40. However, some may have. Records of Native Americans and Aboriginal peoples in the eighteenth and nineteenth centuries show that some individuals lived to reach 100. Therefore, it is possible that their ancestors, who lived in the same way, could have lived to such an age too. The evidence from Egypt suggests that people there lived slightly longer, with ten per cent living beyond 50.

The first years of life were the most dangerous. As many as a quarter of children died before they were five, with a large proportion of those dying before their first birthday. (This wasn't a problem confined to prehistoric societies. In 1899, in Britain, 163 children in every thousand died before their first birthday). The other particularly dangerous stage of life was for women in their late teens and early twenties, when many died in childbirth. This explains why, on average, men lived slightly longer than women.

The mummy of the great Pharaoh Ramesses II, who ruled Egypt from 1279–1212 BCE. Ramesses lived to be 90, an extremely old age. Only eight per cent of pharaohs lived to be 45 although they had the best diet, medical attention and living conditions.

The legacy of ancient Egyptian medicine

Egyptian ideas and methods continued to influence medical developments, even when the Greek and Roman empires became the leading cultures around the Mediterranean. It is easy to think that the three empires followed one another in sequence because each dominated the region in turn. In fact, the Egyptian civilization continued alongside the Greek and Roman empires and there were strong links between them.

Alexander the Great, the great Greek soldier, marked his conquest of Egypt by building a new city at Alexandria in northern Egypt. Alexandria became the most famous center of medical learning in the Greek Empire and it is likely that Egyptian medical texts were copied for the great library there. In the Roman period, around 200 CE, physicians were also visiting the temple at Memphis to read the Egyptian medical texts. Medicine had taken a step forward in ancient Egypt, but it was about to advance much further, thanks to the Greeks.

How good was ancient Egyptian medicine?

The peoples of other lands had a high regard for Egyptian medicine. In the fourteenth century BCE, the rulers of Syria and Assyria sent letters to Egypt asking if they could "borrow" doctors to work at their courts. The great Greek storyteller Homer wrote in *The Odyssey* (*c.* 700 BCE) that "In medical knowledge, the Egyptians leave the rest of the world behind." However, Homer was writing at a time when the Greek civilization was beginning to develop. In the following centuries the Greeks developed their own medical knowledge to such an extent that they left the Egyptians behind.

This carving shows the effects of famine in Egypt. Although Egyptians usually had plenty of food, there were years when the Nile did not flood and the harvests were poor. Then people simply starved unless food had been stored up in previous years. All early societies suffered higher death rates when the harvests failed.

Glossary

Amulet a charm that the wearer believes gives protection from illness

Anaesthetic a drug that induces pain relief, used mostly in preparation for surgery, sometimes making the person unconscious

Anatomy the study of the structure of the human body

Anthrax an infection found in sheep and cattle, which can spread to humans and becomes dangerous if it affects the lungs

Anthropologist a scientist who studies the origin, behavior and physical, social and cultural development of humans

Antibiotic a drug used to treat infections caused by bacteria

Antiseptic a chemical or a natural substance that destroys bacteria and kills infection

Archaeologist someone who studies the past primarily through artifacts—such as buildings, pottery or even human remains

Arthritis (also osteoarthritis) painful swelling of the body's joints

Astrology the study of the stars and planets and how they might influence people's lives

Bacteria the micro-organisms that cause diseases

Cholera an infection that causes extreme diarrhea, dehydration and death

Cistern a storage place for water

Colocynth a plant used in herbal remedies; it resembles the common watermelon but is extremely poisonous if too much is used

Consumption a disease of the lungs that was a major cause of death in the nineteenth and early twentieth centuries; known today as tuberculosis

Cyst a lump or swelling containing liquid or semi-solid matter that can occur in any organ or tissue of the body

Dissection the cutting up and scientific examination of the human body

Dysentery a severe illness causing frequent, fluid bowel movements

Entrails the internal parts of the body, particularly the intestines or bowels

Epidemic a disease affecting a large number of people at once

Epilepsy a nervous disease causing convulsions and loss of consciousness

Galena lead sulphide, a lead and silver ore; the silver has some healing properties

Gangrene the infection of dead human tissue; it can kill the victim unless the tissue is removed

Hallucinations dreams; imagined things or events that are not real

Hieratic script the ancient Egyptians' simplified form of writing, developed by priests

Hieroglyphs the ancient Egyptian form of writing, based on symbols and pictures

Holistic concerned with the whole rather than analysis of the parts

Ibex a species of wild goat

Ice Age a period when much of the northern hemisphere was covered in ice; the last Ice Age ended around 17,000 years ago

Immunity protection against a disease

Incantation a chant or song sung as part of a ceremony or medical cure

Jet a hard and very black carbon stone

Kidneys the organs that filter the blood to cleanse it; they get rid of waste and excess water as urine

Laxative a medicine given to a patient to empty his or her bowels

Leprosy an infection that causes severe damage to the nerves and skin; it eventually leads to death

Liver the organ that acts as the body's chemical factory, regulating the levels of the various chemicals in the blood

Mace a club used in warfare or ceremonies

Natron a mineral used in embalming bodies; it is similar to salt

Physiology the study of how the body works

Placebo a substance containing no medication and given to reinforce a patient's expectation to get well

Pneumonia inflammation of the lungs due to infection

Purge to cleanse the body by taking drugs that make people vomit or empty their bowels

Rabies an acute infection caught from a rabid animal; it affects the nervous system and can often lead to death in humans

Senna the leaves of the cassia plant; they are used as a medicine to empty the bowels

Shekel a silver coin

Smallpox a disease similar to influenza that leads to a severe rash and blisters; it has affected humans for many centuries but became much more dangerous from the eighteenth century onwards, killing 40 per cent of sufferers; it is now extinct

Spleen the organ that removes worn-out blood cells and fights infections

Stagnant sluggish, unmoving

Stibium a silvery-white mineral used in medicines

Sump a pit or well for storing water or other liquids

Trepanning (also trephining) drilling a hole into the skull for medical reasons in order to relieve pressure on the brain

Vertebrae the small bones of the spine

Timeline

Events	Dates All BCE	People
c. 3500 Development of first cities in Mesopotamia, including Ur and Babylon Invention of writing by the Sumerians of Mesopotamia	3500	
c. 3300 Invention of hieroglyphic writing in Egypt	3300	
c. 3100 The first pharaohs united the two kingdoms of Egypt to create one country	3100	
c. 3000 Development of the cities of Harappa and Mohenjo-daro in India	3000	
	2600	Imhotep – born c. 2650; chief adviser to Pharaoh Zozer, (reigned 2630–2611) and was later worshipped as the Egyptian god of medicine Hesy-ra – lived c. 2650; the first recorded doctor, court physician to the Pharaoh and also a dentist
c. 2500 Building of the pyramids at Giza in Egypt Invention of hieratic writing in Egypt	2500	
	2300	Peseshet –the first recorded woman doctor
	2100	Ir-en-akhty –court physician whose tomb records his various medical titles
	1800	Reign of King Hammurabi of Babylon 1792–1750
Period of the writing of the Edwin Smith Papyrus (c. 1550) and the Ebers Papyrus (c. 1500) c. 1500 Cities of Mohenjo-daro and Harrappa were deserted by their peoples	1500	
	1300	Reign of Pharaoh Tutankhamun 1334–1325 Reign of Pharaoh Ramesses II 1279–1212
c. 500 Invasion and conquest of Egyptian kingdom by Persian armies	500	

Further information

Books

Blood and Guts, A Short History of Medicine,
Roy Porter, W. W Norton & Co., 2003
An entertaining, up-to-date history for older readers.

Egyptian Medicine (Shire Egyptology Series)
Colin Morrison Reeves, Shire Publications, 1989

The Empires of Ancient Egypt,
Robert Morkot, BBC Books, 2001

The Atlas of Prehistoric Britain,
John Manley, Oxford University Press, 1989

*Written in Bones: How human remains unlock the
secrets of the dead,* Paul Bahn, Firefly Books, 2003

*The Savage Stone Age & The Awesome Egyptians
(Horrible Histories)*
Terry Deary, Scholastic Hippo, 1999
Entertaining, funny and informative.

*Gods and Goddesses in the Daily Life of the
Ancient Egyptians,* Henrietta McCall, Hodder, 2002

Ancient Egypt (History Beneath Your Feet),
Jane Shuter, Raintree, 1999

Atlas of Ancient Worlds: A Pictoral Atlas, Anne
Millard and Russell Barnett, Dorling Kindersley,
2001

Native American Medicine (Native American Life),
Tamra Orr, Mason Crest Publishers, 2003

*Sun Mother Wakes the World: An Australian
Creation Story,* Diane Wolkstein, Bronwyn
Bancroft, HarperCollins, 2004

*The Songs My Paddle Sings: Native American
Legends,* James Riordan, Michael Foreman,
Pavillion Books, 1997

Tales of Ancient Egypt, Roger Lancelyn Green,
Heather Copley, Puffin Books, 1996

Websites

www.mnsu.edu/emuseum/prehistory/egypt
Part of the museum of Minnesota State
University, covering many aspects of Egyptian
life, including medicine.

www.showcase.netins.net/web/ankh
A highly pictorial, virtual tour of ancient Egypt.

www.mic.ki.se/Egypt.html
A guide to websites on ancient Egypt.

www.nmai.si.edu
Website for the Smithsonian's Museum of the
American Indian.

www.si.edu/resource/faq/nmai/start.htm
Exhibitions, resources, and books on Native
American Life

www.codetalk.fed.us/planet/native.html
List of educational Native American links.

**www.mce.k12tn.net/indians/navigation/native
_american_chart.htm**
A useful chart indicating dress, food, customs,and
tools of different native tribes of North America

**www.brooklynmuseum.org/exhibitions/2003/
egypt-reborn/**
**www.metmuseum.org/Works_of_Art/collection.
asp**
Two world-famous Egyptian collections.

Places to visit

Brooklyn Museum of Art, Brooklyn, New York
www.brooklynmuseum.org
The Metropolitan Museum of Art, New York
www.metmuseum.org

World famous Egyptian collections.

American Museum of Natural History, New York
www.amnh.org

Presents interesting displays about Native
Americans.

**National Museum of the American Indian,
Washington, DC, New York, Maryland**
www.nmai.si.edu

A part of the Smithsonian Institution, these three
museum facilities innovatively present the history, materials, and cultures of Native Americans.

**The Mitchell Museum of the American Indian,
Kendall College, Illinois**
www.mitchellmuseum.org

The only museum in the Chicago area focused
exclusively on the history, culture and arts of
North American native peoples.

California Science Center, Los Angeles, CA
www.casciencectr.org

The West Coast's largest hands-on science center.

St. Louis Science Center, St. Louis, MO
www.slsc.org

Home to a significant medical artifact collection,
originally belonging to the St. Louis Medical
Society.

Index